To

From

Date

Gloria Copeland

Words That Heal

Unless otherwise noted, all scripture is from the *King James Version* of the Bible.

Scripture quotations marked *The Amplified Bible* are from *The Amplified Bible, Old Testament* © 1965, 1987 by The Zondervan Corporation. *The Amplified New Testament* © 1958, 1987 by The Lockman Foundation. Used by permission.

Scripture quotations marked *New International Version* are from *The Holy Bible, New International Version* © 1973, 1978, 1984 by the International Bible Society. Used by permission of Zondervan Publishing House.

Scripture quotations marked *Weymouth* are from *The New Testament in Modern Speech* by Richard Francis Weymouth © 1996 Kenneth Copeland Publications.

Words That Heal

ISBN-10 1-57562-671-3
ISBN-13 978-1-57562-671-0

30-0600

14 13 12 11 10 09

11 10 9 8 7 6

© 2002 Gloria Copeland

Kenneth Copeland Publications
Fort Worth, TX 76192-0001

For more information about Kenneth Copeland Ministries, call 800-600-7395 or visit www.kcm.org.

Designed by Michael Augustat/7th Millennium

KCP Records
The Music of Ministry

Produced by Win Kutz
Vocals: Len Mink
Keyboards: Steve Ingram
Percussion: Gene Glover

Give Thanks
Henry Smith
© 1978 Integrity's Hosanna! Music Inc., ASCAP

Jesus Healed Them All
Steve Ingram
© 1991 Psalmist Covenant Music. ASCAP

I Sing Praises to Your Name
Terry MacAlmon
© 1989 Integrity's Hosanna! Music Inc., ASCAP

I Stand in Awe of You
Mark Altrogge
© 1988 People of Destiny Music/Pleasant Hill Music
Administered by The Harry Fox Agency

Sing Hallelujah to the Lord
Linda Stassen
© 1974 New Song Creations, ASCAP

Rise and Be Healed
Milton Bourgeois
© 1972 Brentwood Benson Music Publishing Co.

God intends for you and me to experience complete healing and total restoration in every area of our lives. After all, we are *His* children and He has made provision for us to have everything we need. He wants us to live in peace. And God's idea of peace or "shalom" is *wholeness in every area, with nothing missing and nothing broken.*

So receive His peace—be made whole—in your body and in your life.

Gloria Copeland

For I am the Lord, I chan

I am the Lord that healeth thee.

—Exodus 15:26

And ye shall serve the Lord your God, and he shall
bless thy bread, and thy water; and I will take sickness
away from the midst of thee...the number of
thy days I will fulfill.

—Exodus 23:25-26

For I am the Lord, I change not....

—Malachi 3:6

Jesus Christ the same yesterday, and today, and for ever.

—Hebrews 13:8

You see God's will and healing from the beginning. In the old covenant and in the new covenant, He's made a way for His people to be well. If they would walk with Him and do what He said, He would take sickness away from the midst of them.

Now it would be absurd for God to provide healing for His people under a lesser covenant and then make a better covenant with better promises (Hebrews 8:6) and there not be any healing provision. God would never do that because He would have to change. He said, "I am the Lord that healeth thee."

—*Gloria Copeland*

Psalm 107:21

The Lord is good to all: and his tender
mercies are over all his works.

—Psalm 145:9

Oh that men would praise the Lord for his
goodness, and for his wonderful works to
the children of men!

—Psalm 107:21

You should be quick to refuse sickness

God has always
made a way for His people to
be well...always. Why is that?
Because He is a good God.

—Gloria Copeland

...Himself took our infirmities,
and bare our sicknesses.
—*Matthew 8:17*

Jesus bore
your sicknesses and carried your
diseases at the same time, and in
the same manner, that He bore
your sins. You are just as free from
sickness and disease as you are
from sin. You should be as quick
to refuse sickness and disease in
your body as you are to refuse sin.
—*Gloria Copeland*

& disease.

But he was wounded
for our transgression.

Surely he hath borne our griefs, and carried our sorrows:
yet we did esteem him stricken, smitten of God, and
afflicted. But he was wounded for our transgressions, he
was bruised for our iniquities: the chastisement of our
peace was upon him; and with his stripes we are healed.

—Isaiah 53:4-5

Who his own self bare our sins in his own body on
the tree, that we, being dead to sins, should live unto
righteousness: by whose stripes ye were healed.

—1 Peter 2:24

"By *whose stripes ye were healed*" is not a promise. It is a fact. It has already taken place. Jesus bore sickness away from you, and by His stripes you were healed.

—*Gloria Copeland*

Christ hath redeemed us from the
curse of the law, being made a curse
for us: for it is written, Cursed is
every one that hangeth on a tree:
That the blessing of Abraham might
come on the Gentiles through Jesus
Christ.... And if ye be Christ's, then
are ye Abraham's seed, and heirs
according to the promise.

—Galatians 3:13-14, 29

Healing Is You

If you put all the wealthy families in the world together, they couldn't give you the inheritance that you have in God. You are an heir through Jesus Christ to the blessing of Abraham. We have an inheritance and we don't have to die to get it. Jesus has already died to get it for us. Jesus bore the curse of the law so that the blessings could come upon you and me.

Jesus has redeemed us from the entire curse—not just from sin, but from the results of sin—from every bad thing that came into this earth as a result of sin.

Inheritance!

The Bible says every sickness and disease is under the curse (Deuteronomy 28:15-68). So you can't have anything today that Jesus didn't Himself pay the price for you to be whole. He took your place and He took your curse!

—Gloria Copeland

Romans 4:17

God...quickeneth the dead, and calleth those things which be not as though they were.
—*Romans 4:17*

If you want to receive something from God, follow His example. Speak it. That's the way faith works.

—*Gloria Copeland*

Make this your confession today: *Jesus has already healed me. I call myself healed! I call myself delivered!*

With God all things are possible.
—*Mark 10:27*

Expect the Impossible

Don't be afraid to expect the impossible. Look for God to do all manner of things in your life today—wonderful things.

Miracles are totally impossible things in the natural realm. Believing God's Word is how God works miracles among us.

—*Gloria Copeland*

And Jesus answering saith unto them, Have faith in God. For verily I say unto you, That whosoever shall say unto this mountain, Be thou removed, and be thou cast into the sea; and shall not doubt in his heart, but shall believe that those things which he saith shall come to pass; he shall have whatsoever he saith.

—Mark 11:22-23

Let us hold fast the profession of our faith without wavering; (for he is faithful that promised).

—Hebrews 10:23

Don't wait until you're sick to start speaking the Word. Start speaking it now.

I'll never forget the first time I realized the importance of speaking the Word. One day as I was sitting at my typewriter typing notes and listening to tapes, I read Mark 11:23. Suddenly, the truth of the last phrase, *"He shall have whatsoever he saith,"* just jumped out at me. The Lord spoke to my heart and said, *In consistency lies the power.*

In Consistency
Lies the Power

It's not just the words you speak when you pray that change things, it's the words you speak all the time!

If what you need is health, go to the Word that tells you, *"By His stripes you were healed,"* and put that in your mouth. Don't talk sickness. Talk health. Don't talk the problem. Talk the answer. Give God words to work with.

—*Gloria Copeland*

Choose Life

I have set before you life and death, blessing and cursing:
therefore choose life, that both thou and thy seed may live.

—Deuteronomy 30:19

Make the decision to live in divine health in the same way that you made the decision to accept Jesus as Savior. Decide to be well!

Just as salvation is being offered to whosoever will, healing is being offered to whosoever will.

Right now by faith confess Jesus as your healer in the same way that you made Him Lord over your life. Make Jesus Lord over your body according to Romans 10:10.

We have to receive what God offers.

—*Gloria Copeland*

According to the Word of God, I confess with my mouth that Jesus is Lord. I confess Him as my healer. I make Him Lord over my body. I believe in my heart that God raised Him from the dead. From this moment, I am saved, healed, made whole and delivered!

Jesus answered and said unto them, Verily
I say unto you, If ye have faith, and doubt
not, ye shall not only do this which is done
to the fig tree, but also if ye shall say unto
this mountain, Be thou removed, and be
thou cast into the sea; it shall be done. And
all things, whatsoever ye shall ask in prayer,
believing, ye shall receive.

—*Matthew 21:21-22*

Believe That You

Receive

God can do anything you can believe for, and you can believe Him for anything you can find in the Word of God. By believing God's Word enough to do it, you and I receive.

—*Gloria Copeland*

Matthew 21:21-22

Submit yourselves
therefore to God. Resist
the devil, and he will
flee from you.

—*James 4:7*

Resist Till Satan Flees

We're continually in a place of resistance to Satan. He's not obligated to flee until we resist him.

If you don't let him talk you out of healing, there's no way he can keep you sick. If you don't let him talk you out of the Word of God, there's nothing he can do in your life to stop you in any way.

—*Gloria Copeland*

Now faith is the substance of things hoped for, the evidence of things not seen.
—*Hebrews 11:1*

Now faith is the assurance (the confirmation, the title deed) of the things [we] hope for, being the conviction of their reality [faith perceiving as real fact what is not revealed to the senses].
—*Hebrews 11:1, The Amplified Bible*

Faith Is Alway

While we look not at the things which are seen, but at the things which are not seen: for the things which are seen are temporal; but the things which are not seen are eternal.
—*2 Corinthians 4:18*

Hebrews 11:1 **Faith** is simply believing what God says rather than what you see or feel here in this natural realm.

You'll find that faith is always now. It is not "God is *going to* do something for me." As long as your words put it off in the future, it will always be in the future because you haven't yet received.

Your faith brings it from the spiritual realm where God lives, into this natural realm where you live.

—Gloria Copeland

NOW

And they overcame him by the
blood of the Lamb, and by the
word of their testimony...

—Revelation 12:11

Blood Was Shed

Nothing But the Blood of Jesus

What can wash away my sins

Nothing but the blood of Jesus

What can make me whole again

Nothing but the blood of Jesus

–Robert Lowery

We're the whole people. We've been made whole by the blood of the Lamb and the word of our testimony.

When it comes to healing, God's Word has to become our word. My testimony is "By His stripes I am healed!"

—Gloria Copeland

for You

We stand in our covenant, Lord, and thank You for the Spirit of God moving in every person who is willing to receive today. Thank You, Lord Jesus, for fixing every single person.

Psalm 91

He that dwelleth in the secret place of the most High shall abide under the shadow of the Almighty. I will say of the Lord, He is my refuge and my fortress: my God; in him will I trust. Surely he shall deliver thee from the snare of the fowler, and from the noisome pestilence...

Because thou hast made the Lord, which is my refuge, even the most High, thy habitation; there shall no evil befall thee, neither shall any plague come nigh thy dwelling...

The Lord Is You

Because he hath set his love upon me, therefore will I deliver him: I will set him on high, because he hath known my name. He shall call upon me, and I will answer him: I will be with him in trouble; I will deliver him, and honour him. With long life will I satisfy him, and show him my salvation.

—Psalm 91: 1-3, 9-10, 14-16

Refuge

Dare to agree with the Word, and healing will be established. The circumstances will follow your action and confession.

—*Gloria Copeland*

Jesus is the healer and He is no respecter of persons. He wants you well, so make this confession:

I receive my wholeness. The Lord is the refuge of my life. The Lord is my healer. I put Him first. I obey Him. I follow His way and I am made whole!

Receive

Mark 11:24

As You Pray

Therefore I say unto you, What things soever ye
desire, when ye pray, believe that ye receive them,
and ye shall have them.
—*Mark 11:24*

To get results, you must believe
you receive your healing *when you pray*—not
after you are well.

—*Gloria Copeland*

The Word
God's

My son, attend to my words;
incline thine ear unto my sayings. Let them not depart from
thine eyes; keep them in the
midst of thine heart. For they
are life unto those that find
them, and health to all their flesh.

—*Proverbs 4:20-22*

Whether you are well or sick, you need the healing scriptures continually deposited into your heart. So when sickness does try to come and attach itself to your body, faith is in you and you're strong. You can say with faith, "No, devil, you're not putting that on me. I'm healed."

Medicine

This constant receiving of the Word of Life is the way you live in divine health.

When we feed on the Word of God and, as Proverbs 4 says, keep God's Word going in our eyes and in our ears so that it stays in our heart, that Word is life and health to all our flesh.

In Proverbs 4, the Hebrew word for health means *medicine*. God's Word is medicine to all of our flesh.

If you will learn to take that medicine daily, whether you have a pain or not, you can stay well. It will be as hard for you to get sick as it once was for you to get well. Symptoms might come occasionally, but when they do come, you know what to do about it, you're strong in the Lord and you have faith because "faith cometh by hearing, and hearing by the Word of God" (Romans 10:17).

Now that's the way we ought to live—taking God's medicine every day, when we feel good and when we feel bad.

The thing about God's medicine is, the more you take, the better and the stronger you feel and are.

—*Gloria Copeland*

Verily I say unto you,
Whosoever shall not receive
the kingdom of God as a little
child shall in no wise enter therein.

—Luke 18:17

You Can't Overdose on the Word!

Take a big dose of God's medicine. It's going to be easy for you to get healed. Your faith will just rise up in you, if you will come like a little child.

If you sit back and argue and want to debate, I can't give you any promise. But if you will just receive the Word of God like a little child, you will receive your healing today.

—Gloria Copeland

Made Whole...

Beloved, I wish above all
things that thou mayest
prosper and be in health,
even as thy soul prospereth.

—3 John 2

Spirit, Sou

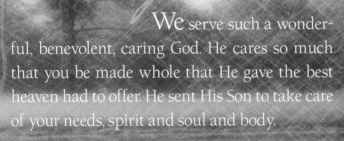

3 John 2

We serve such a wonder-
ful, benevolent, caring God. He cares so much
that you be made whole that He gave the best
heaven had to offer. He sent His Son to take care
of your needs, spirit and soul and body.

& Body

No part of your life has been overlooked. Bible
peace means nothing missing, nothing broken!

—Gloria Copeland

Cast not away therefore
your confidence, which
hath great recompense of
reward. For ye have need of
patience, that, after ye have
done the will of God, ye
might receive the promise.

—*Hebrews 10:35-36*

Do not allow your fearless confidence in God's Word to be snatched away from you by Satan. This is walking by faith and not by sight. Refuse to believe anything but God's Word. God's Word is the last word!

—*Gloria Copeland*

Confident
Expectation

How God anointed Jesus of Nazareth with the Holy Ghost and with power:
who went about doing good, and healing all that were oppressed
of the devil; for God was with him.

—Acts 10:38

If you want to see what the Father is like, look and see what Jesus did when He was on the earth. He said He only did that which He saw the Father do, and He only said what He heard from the Father. He went about doing good. Healing is good. God is good. You can trust Him.

—Gloria Copeland

Acts 10:38

Showing the
Father's Love

Is any sick among you? let him call for the elders of the church;
and let them pray over him, anointing him with oil in the name of the Lord:
And the prayer of faith shall save the sick, and the Lord shall raise him up;
and if he have committed sins, they shall be forgiven him. Confess your
faults one to another, and pray one for another, that ye may be healed. The
effectual fervent prayer of a righteous man availeth much.

—James 5:14-16

And great multitudes came unto
him, having with them those that
were lame, blind, dumb, maimed,
and many others, and cast them
down at Jesus' feet;
and he healed them.

—Matthew 15:30

Vessels

His

And these signs shall follow them that believe; In my name shall they cast o
devils; they shall speak with new tongues; They shall take up serpents; and
they drink any deadly thing, it shall not hurt them; they shall lay hands
on the sick, and they shall recover.

—Mark 16:17-18

People are still getting healed, just like they did when Jesus was in His ministry in His flesh. Jesus is still in His ministry. It's in His Body, and you are the Body of the Lord Jesus Christ. That's why healing is just as available today as it was when Jesus walked the earth.

Nothing changed when He left earth and sat down at the right hand of the Father. People still brought all their sick, and they were still all healed, when they came to the Body of Christ.

# of Healing

And he sent them to preach the kingdom of God, and to heal the sick.
—*Luke 9:2*

The same Spirit that was on Jesus during His earth ministry, the Holy Spirit, is on you today in Christ Jesus. That is why you can lay hands on the sick and they will recover. It does not matter who you are. It is who is in you and on you that does the works and gets people healed.

—*Gloria Copeland*

God's

Life in the Word

God watches over His Word to perform it. His presence is ever in His Word to bring it to pass.

Word Is Alive!

It is God's Word to you now. This Word about healing has the power in it to accomplish the purpose for which it is sent—the healing of your body.

It is just the same as if Jesus called you by name and said, *"I bore your sicknesses and carried your diseases and by My stripes you are healed."*

When you have seen it in the Word, you have heard from God! Your healing would be no more valid and sure if Jesus appeared to you in person and spoke these words.

—Gloria Copeland

...am alert and active, watching over My word to perform it.
—Jeremiah 1:12, The Amplified Bible

...e sent his word, and healed them, and elivered them from their destructions.
—Psalm 107:20

You Can
Have It Al

Psalm 103:1-5

Bless the Lord, O my soul: and all that is within me, bless his holy name. Bless the Lord, O my soul, and forget not all his benefits: who forgiveth all thine iniquities; who healeth all thy diseases; who redeemeth thy life from destruction; who crowneth thee with lovingkindness and tender mercies; who satisfieth thy mouth with good things; so that thy youth is renewed like the eagle's.

—*Psalm 103:1-5*

If I had to choose between the New Birth and healing, I would choose the New Birth because that is eternal and the body is temporary.

But I don't have to choose! In fact, it is not scriptural to choose. Psalm 103 says, *Forget not all his benefits*. It doesn't say choose one. It says don't forget any of them.

—*Gloria Copeland*

Matthew 18:18

Stand Up for What's Yours

Verily I say unto you,
Whatsoever ye shall
bind on earth shall be
bound in heaven: and
whatsoever ye shall
loose on earth shall be
loosed in heaven.

—Matthew 18:18

Jesus gave the Church authority, but we have to take it.

The reason it doesn't work automatically for us, even though it's the will of God and Jesus bought and paid for it, is because there is an outlaw in the world named Satan.

If you don't enforce the law in the spirit realm in your family, sickness and disease will continue to reign there. You have to take the Word and the Name of Jesus, and enforce it.

Criminals don't adhere to the law unless they're forced to. Satan will continue to rob and plunder unless you enforce the Word of God on him. That is the law. God is the Most High God—what He says goes!

Just like a policeman would bind a thief to arrest him, we have to bind the devil. We incarcerate him with the Word of God.

Learn to be bold, not timid. Stand up for what belongs to you. Fight the good fight of faith. That is the way you live in divine health.

—Gloria Copeland

And the very God of peace sanctify you wholly; and I pray God your whole spirit and soul and body be preserved blameless unto the coming of our Lord Jesus Christ.

—*1 Thessalonians 5:23*

Being confident of this very thing, that he which hath begun a good work in you will perform it until the day of Jesus Christ.

—*Philippians 1:6*

Kept Intact &

Who satisfieth thy mouth with good things; so that thy youth is renewed like the eagle's.

—*Psalm 103:5*

"The very God of peace sanctify you *wholly*." That means "whole, complete, undamaged and intact."

When I looked up this definition, I got thrilled because I had been using the word *intact* in my prayer for my own well-being. We should keep these words in our mouths all the time. Every day make this declaration by giving God thanksgiving for what He has done.

Undamaged

Lord, I thank You for keeping me intact—spirit, soul and body. I thank You that my youth is renewed like the eagle's. I thank You, Lord, that my mind is sound. I thank You, Lord, that my body is sound. I thank You, Lord, for keeping my body, my spirit and my soul strong and intact, undamaged and complete all the days of my life. Amen!

Talk words like that. Talk healing when you feel good. Talk healing when you feel bad. Talk the Word of God and let the life of God flow out of you to keep you well and strong.

—Gloria Copeland

Restored

For I will restore health unto
thee, and I will heal thee of thy
wounds, saith the Lord.
—*Jeremiah 30:17*

The law of the Lord is perfect,
restoring the [whole] person...
—*Psalm 19:7*, The Amplified Bible

Lord, we come today to let Your healing anointing flow and to worship You. We're so grateful that You bore our sickness and carried our diseases. You bore our sins and You bore the chastisement of our peace so that we can be whole, complete and every area of our life redeemed. We thank You for it and we praise You, Mighty God.

to Enjoy Life

We believe, Lord, that You are the Healer, and we look to You for the health and restoration of our bodies. We recognize and know that it's from You, and Your Spirit does the work.

Lord, there's nothing too hard for You. It's a little thing to open blind eyes. It's a little thing to You, Lord, to restore a whole leg, to put an arm where there was no arm, to replace a kidney or give somebody a new heart. We just open up our faith and our receiving, Lord, for wholeness today, for every person. You paid the price for every one of us to be healed and whole, and we give You honor in Jesus' Name. Amen.

—Gloria Copeland

Deuteronomy 7:15

The Lord will keep you free
from every disease.

—*Deuteronomy 7:15, New International Version*

When Sickness Knocks, Don't Answer

We absolutely have a covenant of healing and immunity from sickness and disease, but we have to put ourselves in a position to receive with our faith, with our mouth.

You might get a miracle, but you can't live on miracles. They are just a band-aid until you can get the Word of God in your heart and stand for your own deliverance. Which is better, to receive a miracle when you are sick or to be well and not need a miracle?

That's the will of God for us, that we live connected to God so that we stay well and healed and stand on the Word of God. When sickness and disease comes, you don't let it in. You resist it and stand against it with God's Word in your heart and in your mouth.

—*Gloria Copeland*

But if the Spirit of him that raised up
Jesus from the dead dwell in you, he
that raised up Christ from the dead
shall also quicken your mortal bodies
by his Spirit that dwelleth in you.

—Romans 8:11

Given Life by

If the Spirit of Him who raised up Jesus from the dead is dwelling
in you, He who raised up Christ from the dead will give life also to
your mortal bodies through His Spirit dwelling in you.

—Romans 8:11, Weymouth

That's not talking about the resurrection. That's talking about every day that you live. The Spirit—the life of the Anointed One in you—will give life to your mortal body. When your body is in need, the Spirit of God in you gives you life.

The Word is life and health. The Spirit of God brings that Word up in us. He quickens it to us, and that's our medicine. That's what we're to live on daily. That's how we keep our body healed—by the Spirit of God giving life and quickening, or making alive, our mortal bodies.

—Gloria Copeland

His Spirit

And this is the confidence that we have in

him, that, if we ask any thing according to

his will, he heareth us: And if we know that

he hear us, whatsoever we ask, we know that

we have the petitions that we desired of him.

—1 John 5:14-15

Once you find out the will of God concerning healing, you know how to pray. You don't pray, "If it be Thy will." There is no faith in that prayer where healing is concerned. You have faith from knowing what God's will is from what He has already said.

Faith begins where the will of God is known.

You rebuke sickness in Jesus' Name and command your body to be healed. Believe you receive your healing and thank God for it.

—*Gloria Copeland*

His Will Is to Heal

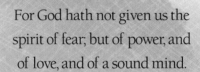

For God hath not given us the
spirit of fear; but of power, and
of love, and of a sound mind.

—*2 Timothy 1:7*

Timothy 1:7

Glory to God! We have a sound mind! Love keeps us that way. Love has peace with it.

People who have depression think about themselves.

But the love of God will put your mind on somebody else.

If depression tries to come on you, begin to look to someone to show love. Begin to help other people. Start giving out of yourself.

t Peace in
God's Love

Keep the commandment of love and you'll do well in life. You'll walk in the blessing of God, and you'll have peace.

—*Gloria Copeland*

Life

When you operate in the kingdom of God, it doesn't matter if the doctor says, "terminal," because you're not depending on him. You're depending on God and the laws of His kingdom to put you over.

Without Limits

For the law of the Spirit of life in Christ Jesus hath made me free from the law of sin and death.

—Romans 8:2

What does that do? It lifts you out of the limitations of this life. You don't have to live under the laws of sin and death anymore after you make Jesus Christ the Lord of your life. You don't have to live in the kingdom of darkness. The law of life that's in Christ Jesus makes you free from the law of sin and death.

—Gloria Copeland

John 8:32

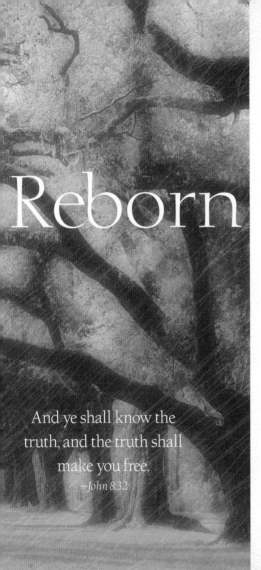

Reborn Free

It's up to us to obey God if we want to walk supernaturally free. We have a manual of freedom that tells us what to do, what to say and how to act.

It's foolish for us as born-again, Spirit-filled Christians to spend our time doing what the world does when we could spend time doing what God says and be totally free. It takes a lot of time to be sick. It takes a lot of time to be in bondage. We could spend that time in the Word and live a happy, fulfilled, peaceful, whole life all the time. That is the will of God.

—Gloria Copeland

And ye shall know the truth, and the truth shall make you free.

—John 8:32

The thief cometh not, but for to steal, and to kill,
and to destroy: I am come that they might have life, and
that they might have it more abundantly.

—John 10:10

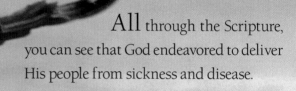

John 10:10

All through the Scripture, you can see that God endeavored to deliver His people from sickness and disease.

Sickness comes from the devil. He is the author of it. It is the result of sin.

Know Your Enemy

Get hold of the fact that good things come from God and bad things come from the devil. Don't get them mixed up. God is not doing bad things and the devil is not doing good things. Draw the line in your thinking and don't ever get confused again.

—*Gloria Copeland*

Again I say unto you, That if two of you shall agree on
earth as touching any thing that they shall ask, it shall
be done for them of my Father which is in heaven.

—*Matthew 18:19*

Agree...
It Shall Be

Let's pray & agree!

Father, we agree as touching sickness and disease and infirmity and anything that's missing or broken. We agree that it is healed today. We thank You, Lord, that You are in our midst to heal every person of every sickness and disease or condition that is not in line with divine health.

Say, I agree on it! I touch this with my faith! In Jesus' Name, we are in agreement concerning the healing, the deliverance, the wholeness of every person reading these words, wherever they are in the earth at this moment. In Jesus' Name. Amen!

—Gloria Copeland

Start Talking...

[Not in your own strength] for it is God Who is all the while effectually at work in you—energizing and creating in you the power and desire—both to will and to work for His good pleasure and satisfaction and delight.
—*Philippians 2:13*, The Amplified Bible

Let the weak say, I am strong.
—*Joel 3:10*

Finally, my brethren,
be strong in the Lord,
and in the power
of his might.
—*Ephesians 6:10*

Strength

Fear thou not; for I am with thee: be not dismayed; for I am thy God: I will strengthen thee; yea, I will help thee; yea, I will uphold thee with the right hand of my righteousness.
—*Isaiah 41:10*

It's feeding on God's Word that makes you strong and keeps you strong. If you are weak in your body, have a list of strength scriptures and take them like medicine. Take them with your eyes. Take them with your ears. Put them in your mouth! Start talking strength, health and peace.

There are not any miracle drugs that will do what the Word of God will do. It doesn't have any side effects and you can't get an overdose. You can take all you want!

—*Gloria Copeland*

Health & Peace.

And now let the weak say I am strong
Let the poor say I am rich
Because of what the Lord has done
Give thanks

—*Henry Smith*

Be anxious for nothing, but in everything by
prayer and supplication, with thanksgiving, let your
requests be made known to God; and the peace of God,
which surpasses all understanding, will guard your
hearts and minds through Christ Jesus.
—*Philippians 4:6-7, New International Version*

Now thanks be unto God, which always
causeth us to triumph in Christ....
—*2 Corinthians 2:14*

But thanks be to God, which giveth us the victory
through our Lord Jesus Christ.
—*1 Corinthians 15:57*

Giving thanks unto the Father, which hath made
us meet to be partakers of the inheritance of the saints
in light: Who hath delivered us from the power of
darkness, and hath translated us into the
kingdom of his dear Son.
—*Colossians 1:12-13*

God Gave Us the Victory

When I pray for something, then if I mention it to the Lord again, I'll mention it to Him in thanksgiving. I'll say, "Lord, I thank You for my healing." I don't ask Him over and over to heal me.

If I were to give you a gift, what would be the next thing you should do?

Thank me.

Should you come back tomorrow and ask me why I didn't give you a gift? No.

Why do I thank the Lord? Because I've already believed I received. He's already given it to me in His Word. I'm going to act like I have it. When I act like I have it, it's going to manifest in my life. Glory to God!

—Gloria Copeland

Proverbs 17:22

The Joy of the Lord Is You

A merry heart doeth good
like a medicine: but a broken spirit
drieth the bones.
—*Proverbs 17:22*

The joy of the Lord is your strength.
—*Nehemiah 8:10*

One day I was reading Proverbs 4 as I was preparing for a healing service in the Philippines. I looked out the window and there was a big fountain shooting way up in the air. The Lord said, *That's the way it is in your spirit.*

Strength.

He said there's water coming out of the mouth of that fountain just like there's life coming out of us if we're born again and filled with the Holy Ghost. As long as there's an overflow, you could put a piece of trash there and it would just flow out. Nothing would stick to it.

It is very difficult for anything to stick to somebody who has a merry heart and a merry outlook on life. It's hard to make a person sick when they have the joy of the Lord flowing out of them.

We ought to stay so full of the Word and the life of God that sickness and disease couldn't even come close to us.

—*Gloria Copeland*

Walking

n the Light of God

What gives you confidence toward God? Knowing that you are doing what He tells you to do.

Great faith comes when you have great assurance that you are walking in the light that you have, and you are seeking God for more light. When you go before God, you know there is not anything that you are withholding from Him, and it is easy to expect Him to withhold nothing from you.

—*Gloria Copeland*

Beloved, if our heart condemn us not, then have we confidence toward God. And whatsoever we ask, we receive of him, because we keep his commandments, and do those things that are pleasing in his sight.
—*1 John 3:21-22*

God's Medicine

My son, attend to my words;
incline thine ear unto my sayings.
–Proverbs 4:20

To be spoken by mouth three times a day until faith comes,
then once a day to maintain faith. If circumstances grow worse,
double the dosage. There are no harmful side effects.
–Charles Capps, God's Creative Power for Healing

Exodus 15:26	*Mark 10:27*
Exodus 23:25	*Mark 11:22-24*
Deuteronomy 7:14-15	*Mark 16:14-18*
Deuteronomy 28:1-14	*John 10:10*
Deuteronomy 30:19-20	*Romans 4:16-21*
1 Kings 8:56	*Romans 8:2, 11*
Psalm 91:9-10	*2 Corinthians 10:3-5*
Psalm 91:14-16	*2 Corinthians 4:18*
Psalm 103:1-5	*Galatians 3:13-14, 29*
Psalm 107:8, 19-21	*Ephesians 6:10-17*
Psalm 118:17	*Philippians 1:6*
Proverbs 4:20-24	*Philippians 2:13*
Isaiah 40:29, 31	*Philippians 4:6-7*
Isaiah 41:10	*2 Timothy 1:7*
Isaiah 53:4-5	*Hebrews 10:23*
Jeremiah 1:12	*Hebrews 10:35-36*
Jeremiah 30:17	*Hebrews 11:11*
Joel 3:10	*Hebrews 13:8*
Nahum 1:9	*James 5:14-16*
Matthew 8:2-3	*1 Peter 2:24*
Matthew 8:16-17	*1 John 3:21-22*
Matthew 18:18-19	*1 John 5:14-15*
Matthew 21:21	*3 John 2*
Mark 9:23	*Revelation 12:11*

A Prayer of
Thanksgiving
for Wholeness

Psalm 91:15-16 says, *"He shall call upon me, and I will answer him: I will be with him in trouble; I will deliver him, and honour him. With long life will I satisfy him, and show him my salvation."*

The Greek word translated *salvation* denotes "deliverance, preservation, material and temporal deliverance from danger and apprehension, pardon, protection, liberty, health, restoration, soundness and wholeness."

The Hebrew word *shalom* for salvation means almost the same thing— "completeness, wholeness, peace, health, welfare, safety, soundness, tranquility."

Your salvation is everything it takes to make your life complete.

Just as sure as it is God's will for you to be born again and for sin to be eradicated out of your spirit, it is God's will for you to be whole completely, from the top of your head to the soles of your feet.

The same sacrifice, the same Savior...Jesus paid the price for every sickness and every disease. The bill's been paid. The work's been done. The healing has been bought.

The whole curse was taken upon Jesus.

Everything Adam lost in the Fall, Jesus got back for us in redemption.

At the same time He bore our sins, He bore our sickness and carried our diseases.

We are healed. Now it's up to us to receive it.

Lord, we just praise You for Your goodness. We thank You, Lord, that every person reading this is being healed today, delivered today, made sound today, spirit, soul and body. We thank You, Lord, for giving us Your Son to be our Savior. We receive Him as our Savior and our Healer. We receive Him as our Deliverer. We are saved. We are healed. We are delivered. You so loved us that You gave Your only Son for us, that we might have life. We thank You for Your mighty goodness to us, Lord! When You gave us Your Son, You gave us all good things. And so we worship You today, Lord. And we thank You for doing miracles and giving wholeness. We thank You for total deliverance and total healing.

—*Gloria Copeland*

A Prayer of Healing

If you want to pray the prayer to receive healing, or if you don't need healing, but you just want to release your faith for health, you can pray and receive right now.

Jesus is the healer. All you have to do is say and do. Say, "He is our healer," and believe the Word of God and expect.

If you are willing to receive, if you believe the Word of God and faith is in your heart, it will be easy for you to receive.

Lift your hands to the Lord, pray this in faith, and mean it with your whole heart. Just come simply, not questioning the Word, but believing.

The Gospel that I have heard is the power of God unto my salvation.
I confess Jesus Christ as the Lord over my life—spirit, soul, body. I receive the power
of God to make me whole, sound, delivered, saved and healed now. I act on the Word
of God and receive. I receive the power of God.

Sickness, disease and pain, I resist you in the Name of Jesus.
You are not the will of God. I enforce the Word of God on you.
I will not tolerate you in my life. Leave my presence!
I will never allow you back.

I have been healed. I have been made sound. Jesus made
me whole. My days of sickness and disease are over.

I am the saved, I am the healed, and the power of sickness has been
forever broken over my life. Jesus bore my sickness. Jesus bore my weakness.
Jesus bore my pain and I am free.

Sickness shall no longer lord it over me. Sin shall no longer lord
it over me. Fear shall no longer lord it over me. Evil addictions
shall no longer lord it over me.

I have been redeemed from the curse and I receive the blessing.
I proclaim my freedom in Jesus' Name. Today the gospel is the power of God
to me unto salvation. I receive the gospel. I act on the gospel and I am
made whole, nothing missing, nothing broken, in the
Name of the Lord Jesus Christ. Amen!

—*Gloria Copeland*

Prayer for
Salvation & Baptism
in the Holy Spirit

Heavenly Father, I come to You in the Name of Jesus. Your Word says, "Whosoever shall call on the name of the Lord shall be saved" (Acts 2:21). I am calling on You. I pray and ask Jesus to come into my heart and be Lord over my life according to Romans 10:9-10: "If thou shalt confess with thy mouth the Lord Jesus, and shalt believe in thine heart that God hath raised him from the dead, thou shalt be saved. For with the heart man believeth unto righteousness; and with the mouth confession is made unto salvation." I do that now. I confess that Jesus is Lord, and I believe in my heart that God raised Him from the dead.

I am now reborn! I am a Christian—a child of Almighty God! I am saved!
You also said in Your Word, "If ye then, being evil, know how to give good
gifts unto your children: HOW MUCH MORE shall your heavenly Father
give the Holy Spirit to them that ask him?" (Luke 11:13). I'm also asking
You to fill me with the Holy Spirit. Holy Spirit, rise up within me as
I praise God. I fully expect to speak with other tongues as You give
me the utterance (Acts 2:4). In Jesus' Name. Amen!

Begin to praise God for filling you with the Holy Spirit. Speak those words and syllables you receive—not in your own language, but the language given to you by the Holy Spirit. You have to use your own voice. God will not force you to speak. Don't be concerned with how it sounds. It is a heavenly language!

Continue with the blessing God has given you and pray in the spirit every day. You are a born-again, Spirit-filled believer. You'll never be the same!

Find a good church that boldly preaches God's Word and obeys it. Become part of a church family who will love and care for you as you love and care for them. We need to be connected to each other. It increases our strength in God. It's God's plan for us. Make it a habit to watch the *Believer's Voice of Victory* television broadcast and become a doer of the Word, who is blessed in his doing (James 1:22-25).

Other Products to Help You Receive Your Healing

Books by Gloria Copeland

And Jesus Healed Them All
God's Prescription for Divine Health
God's Will for Your Healing
Harvest of Health

Audio Resources by Gloria Copeland

Be Made Whole—Live Long, Live Healthy
God Is a Good God
God Wants You Well
Healing Confessions (CD and minibook)
Healing School

DVD Resources by Gloria Copeland

Be Made Whole—Live Long, Live Healthy
Know Him As Healer

Books By Kenneth Copeland

You Are Healed

Books Co-Authored by Kenneth and Gloria Copeland

Healing Promises
One Word From God Can Change Your Health

Audio Resources by Kenneth Copeland

Healing—Is It God's Will?
You Are Healed!
Taking Authority Over the Curse

Audio Resources by Kellie Copeland Swisher

And Jesus Healed Them All—Healing Praise
for Your Children
And Jesus Healed Them All Tote
Children's Healing Confession Book and Music CD

*Available in Spanish